Bubba's Egg

by Jeryl Christmas

Photography by Lindsay Christmas Rowe

This Book Belongs To

_____

This book is dedicated to
my free-spirited, nature-loving
grandson, Jackson, also known as
Bubba.

Bubba has an **EGG**-friend

that needs a lot of care.

He must be very gentle

when he takes it anywhere.

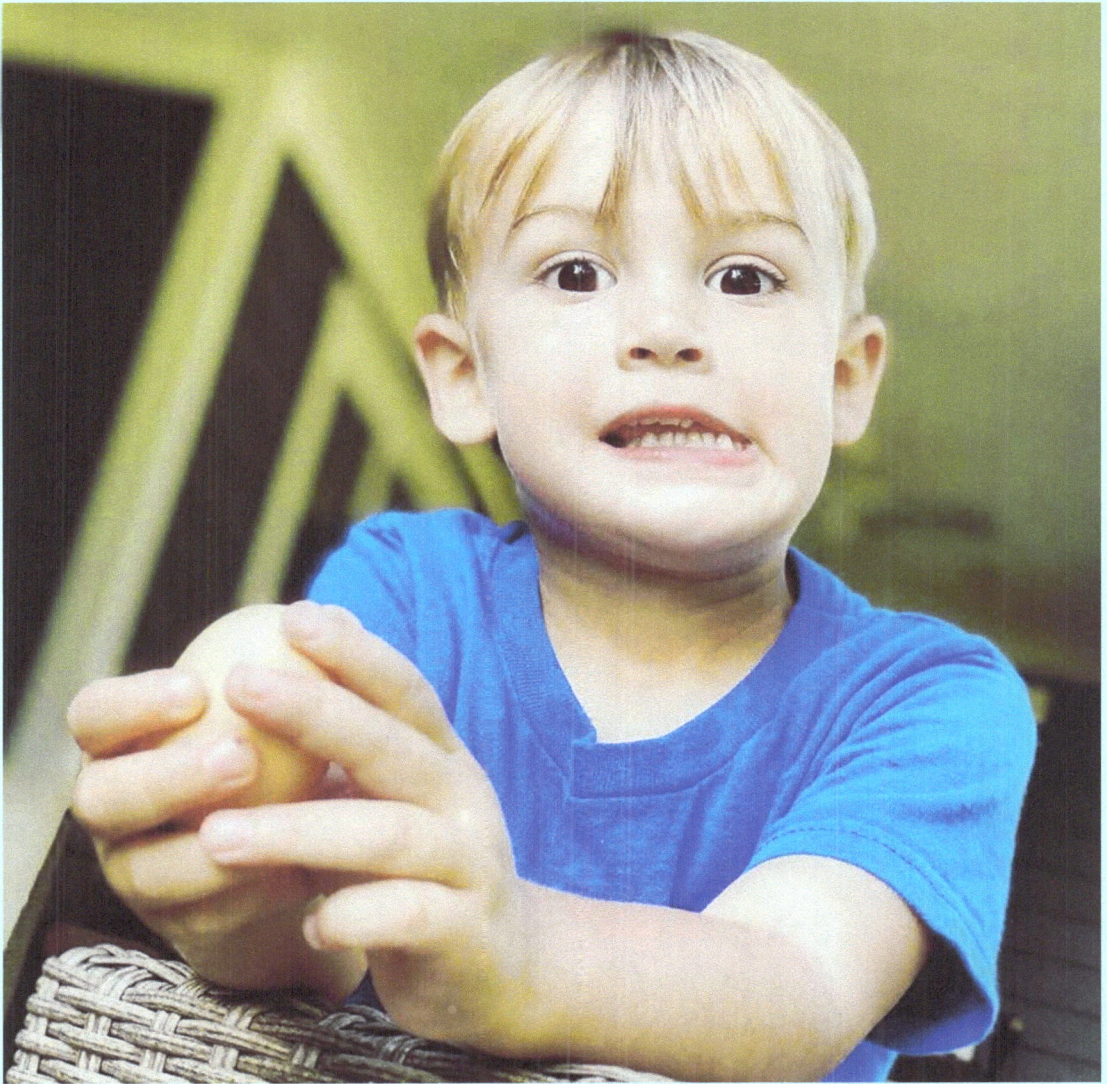

His friend is very fragile

so to others he will tell,

"My egg is really special.

I **CANNOT** break its shell!"

How did this friendship happen?

Let's rewind for just a bit.

Bubba's **NOT** a city boy.

Here's where he'd rather sit.

Caterpillar hunting

is his favorite thing to do.

"Critter-creeping" is a skill

that's mastered by a few.

He loves to walk with Mommy.

That's really what he likes—

early in the morning

holding hands while taking hikes.

They go to see the chickens

that Paw Paw likes to raise

and hope to see a setting hen

with the egg she lays.

He finds the perfect one

and takes it to the deck.

He puts it in a basket

that he can often check.

Such a valuable possession

is a treasure for this boy.

The simple things in life

always bring the greatest joy.

He asks if this nice rooster

would like to meet his friend

or "**COCK-A-DOODLE-DO**"

a greeting to extend.

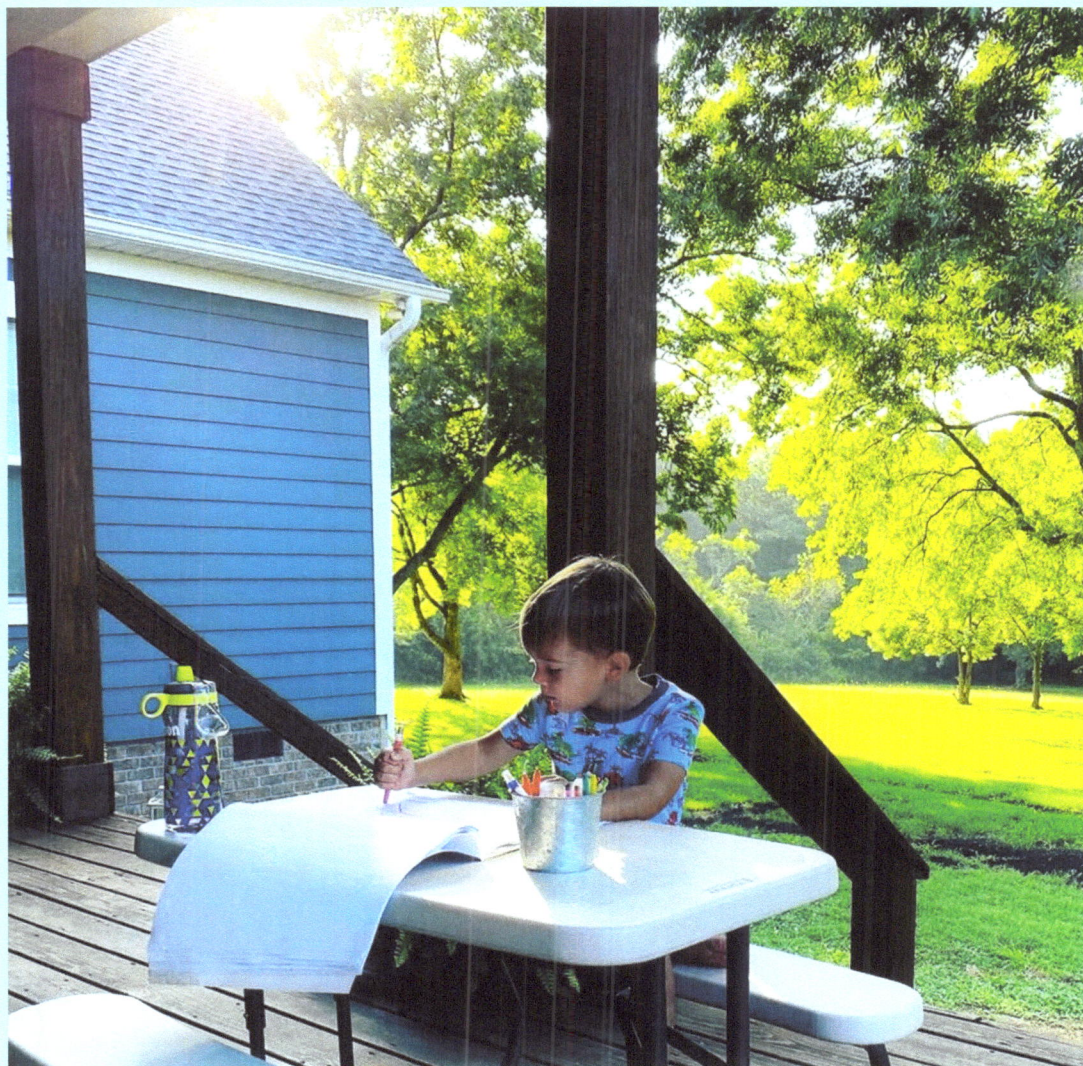

He draws a lot of pictures

of places they might go.

Imagination never ends.

It should **ALWAYS** grow!

Road trips will be taken,

much to their delight,

buckled in so safely

with their seat belts on just right.

WHEELIES in the backyard!

They watch Dad from their seat.

Mommy says what Daddy does

Bubba can't repeat.

Later it is bath time.

Making sure that all is well,

he sneaks a peek or two

to take a look at his friend's shell.

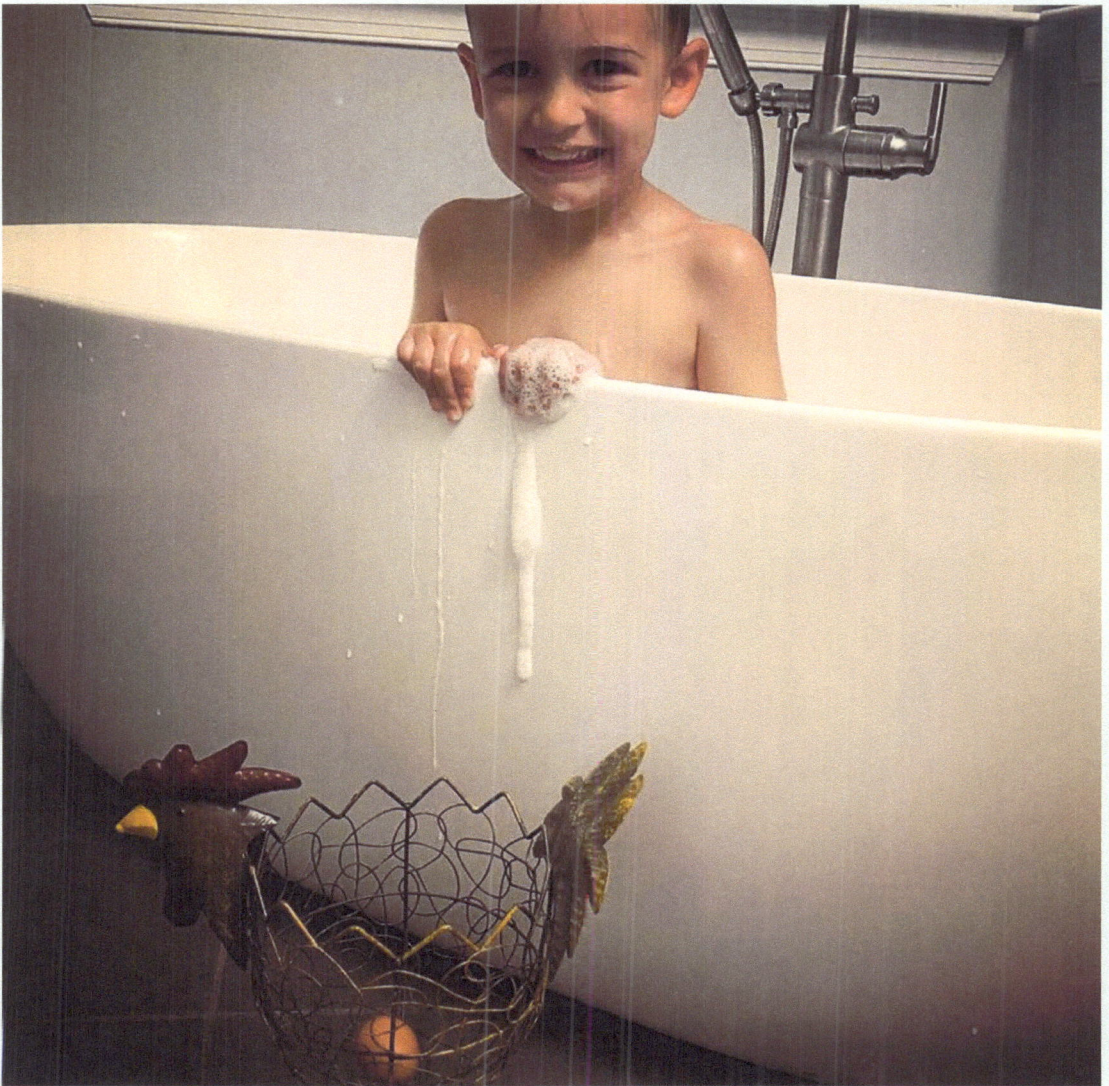

Not a single crack is found.

He's really very proud.

He'd like to shout in pure delight,

but that would be too loud.

Those hands on Mommy's face,

her lips upon his head,

always seem to come before

his time to go to bed.

But Bubba doesn't mind it

since he has his special friend.

There really is no better way

for this fun day to end.

He knows that in the morning,

he'll start a brand new day

of hunting, hiking, hugging,

and lots of things to play.

His mommy tells him stories

while sitting in the shade

about a little boy

and the special friend he made.

He thinks back on those times.

Then later he will see

a surprise from his sis.

Can you guess what it might be?

Beside a broken shell

was a **CHICK** that he could touch.

He loves his brand new friend

so very, very much!

What else will he discover

that's right before his eyes—

things this little boy will see

before he gets **MAN**-size?

But even though he's growing up,

now at the age of three,

his special sense of **WONDER**

will keep his spirit free!

THE END